THE
BALD EAGLE

BY
JANA McCONOUGHEY

EDITED BY
DR. HOWARD SCHROEDER
**Professor in Reading and Language Arts
Dept. of Elementary Education
Mankato State University**

PRODUCED AND DESIGNED BY
BAKER STREET PRODUCTIONS
Mankato, MN

CRESTWOOD HOUSE
Mankato, Minnesota

LIBRARY OF CONGRESS CATALOGING IN PUBLICATION DATA

McConoughey, Jana
  The bald eagle.

  (Wildlife, habits and habitat)
  SUMMARY: Describes the physical characteristics, habits, and natural
environment of the bald eagle.
  1. Bald eagle--Juvenile literature. (1. Bald eagle. 2. Eagles) I. Title. II.
Series.
QL696.F32M35   598'.916   83-5162
ISBN 0-89686-218-6 (lib. bdg.)

International Standard Book Number:	Library of Congress Catalog Card Number:
Library Binding 0-89686-218-6	83-5162

ILLUSTRATION CREDITS:

Sean Morgan/F-Stop: Cover, 27
National Park Service: 5
Jerg Kroener: 7, 8, 14, 21, 41
Lynn Rogers: 11, 23, 34, 38-39, 43
Bob & Clara Calhoun/Bruce Coleman, Inc.: 13
Jeff Foott/Bruce Coleman, Inc.: 17
Bob Williams: 18, 31, 32, 37
Fish & Wildlife Service: 25, 29
Tom Stack/Tom Stack & Assoc.: 44

CRESTWOOD HOUSE

Hwy. 66 South, Box 3427
Mankato, MN 56002-3427

TABLE OF CONTENTS

INTRODUCTION:

When people think of bounty hunters, they usually think of the ruthless cowboys of the West, who tracked down wanted gunmen and brought them, dead or alive, to the local sheriff for a reward. However, during the early 1900's there was a different type of bounty hunter in North America. These men hunted not other men, but bald eagles.

During this time, the fishing industries of Alaska and northern Canada were not doing too well. To make matters worse, bald eagles had acquired the habit of perching on the poles of fish traps that were used by the salmon fishermen. This caused the salmon to panic and beat against the traps until they were too mangled to sell.

In 1917, a bounty was placed on eagles across upper North America. Any man who had a pair of eagle feet could trade them in for fifty cents. In 1923, the bounty on eagles was increased to one dollar. Thousands of eagles fell prey to the guns of bounty hunters.

In the 1950's the United States Fish and Wildlife Service decided too many eagles were being killed. To get around the problem, the service designed new traps for the salmon fishermen which had spiked poles. The spikes prevented the bald eagles from

A bald eagle perches in a tree in Alaska.

landing on the traps and scaring the salmon. The birds were no longer a problem for the fishermen. By 1955, the bounty on eagles was repealed, but not before over 100,000 birds had been killed.

CHAPTER ONE:

Though many people have not seen a bald eagle, it is probably the best known bird in North America. Its picture appears on money in the United States, and its figure stands atop flag poles. Scientists call it *Haliaeetus leucocephalus.*

There are actually two races of bald eagles in North America. There is a southern race and a northern race. The northern race is found mostly in Alaska and Canada. The southern race is found mainly south of the Canada - United States border. The northern race is slightly larger. Eagles living in Alaska are the largest eagles in North America. Other than size, though, the differences between the two races are too small to mention. Even scientists have trouble telling the two types apart. The two races are usually thought of as just one type of bird.

An impressive looking bird

The bald eagle is a large bird. The females are usually larger than the males. They measure three to three and a half feet (1 m) long when they are fully grown. Their wingspan (distance from wing tip to wing tip when the wings are outstretched) is one of the longest of all birds. A female's wingspan can be more than seven feet (2.13 m)! She can weigh ten to

A mature bald eagle.

sixteen pounds (4.5-7.3 kg). Male bald eagles are as much as seven inches (18 cm) shorter than the females and two to three pounds (.9-1.4 kg) lighter. Their wingspan may only be six and a half feet (1.98 m) across.

Until it is four or five years old, the bald eagle does not have a white head.

The bald eagle is an impressive looking bird. It is not bald, as the name suggests. But the pure white feathers that cover its entire head make it look bald from a distance. The rest of its body — except the tail, which is also white — is covered with dark brown feathers. The bald eagle does not have this color pattern, though, until it is four to five years old. Before that time it is brown, with flecks of white over much of its body.

A skilled flyer and hunter

One remarkable thing about a bald eagle is its flying ability. Despite its large size, the eagle is very graceful in the air. Its long, broad wings are well adapted for soaring. The feathers on its wings are slotted at the tips. This helps stabilize the eagle while flying, giving it a smooth ride even in very windy weather.

In addition to its excellent flying abilities, the bald eagle has very good eyesight. It can see details that a human eye cannot see. For example, a soaring eagle can see a rabbit on the ground so far away that a human could not see it without using binoculars. Eagles also have very good depth perception (the ability to judge how far away an object is from the eye). This is important for the eagle, as it swoops down from the sky toward its prey.

The bald eagle has more than good eyesight, though, to help it catch its prey. It has talons, or feet, with long, sharp claws that can grab onto its prey. These talons are strong enough to hold the prey as the bird flies through the air. The bald eagle also has a thick, hooked bill that can tear food into bite sized pieces. All of these things make the eagle an excellent hunter.

Home of the eagle

Much of the eagle's diet consists of fish. For that reason eagles build their nests near lakes and rivers. A towering pine that reaches over 120 feet (37 m) into the air is the perfect nest site for an eagle. From their high nests they can watch the ground and water beneath them for prey. An eagle's nest is also very large. It takes a large, strong tree to support it.

Some eagles live where there are not many trees. These birds build their nests on cliffside ledges which overlook the water. These cliffside nests are sometimes seen in Alaska and Canada.

A nasty bird?

Many times the eagle steals its food from other birds, such as the osprey. The osprey is a fish-eating bird that is quite a bit smaller than the eagle. A bald eagle will chase an osprey until the smaller bird gives up and drops the fish it has caught. Then the eagle will snatch it up and fly away to eat what should have been the osprey's dinner.

Surprisingly, the bald eagle often picks on birds that are smaller than itself. It rarely picks on anything its own size except for other eagles.

Eagles are not admired for their personalities. But anyone who has seen an eagle in flight is struck with awe by its skill in the air. At mealtime the eagle becomes an aerial acrobat. One cannot help admiring it for the grace and beauty it displays in the sky.

The eagle is a graceful flyer.

CHAPTER TWO:

An unusual courtship

The bald eagle displays amazing flying skills when it hunts for its prey. However, it is during the mating season that this bird shows off its real flying talents. The mating season of the bald eagle begins at different times, depending on where the birds live. Those eagles that breed along the west coast of Canada and the United States, and those around the Great Lakes Region, begin courting in February. Eagles living in the southeast corner of the United States begin courting in March or April.

Eagles do not care about whom their mates are. A young eagle may pair with another eagle that is many years older. Eagles may live to be forty years old, so there can be quite an age difference between mates. An old eagle that has lost its mate will search for a new, and often younger, mate.

The bald eagle has a very unusual courtship routine. During the mating season couples are always together. In the afternoons they fly high into the air. The two birds climb so high into the air that a human eye is barely able to see them. Then one of the birds rolls over and flies upside down in perfect control. The bird stretches its yellow talons out over its stomach as an invitation to its mate. The other bird approaches and the two intertwine their talons and lock them together. Then the two birds spread their wings and cartwheel over and over toward the earth. They tumble through the sky at top speed, and it looks as if they will crash onto the ground. But, in the nick of time, they break apart and fly back up into the sky. The mates continue these acrobatics throughout the mating season.

Building the nest

Eagles do not usually build nests until they have paired with a mate. Until that time, eagles live by

Eagles usually build their nests at the top of a tall tree.

themselves without home or family. When an eagle finally does choose a mate, the two begin the large task of building their new home.

Nest building takes about four days of almost

Both the male and the female help to build the nest.

constant work by the eagles. First, the male flies off to gather sticks that will form the base of the nest. Some sticks he chooses may be six feet (1.8 m) long, and two inches (5 cm) in diameter! He picks these up off the ground by swooping over them and grabbing them with his talons. He doesn't even have to land. The eager nest builder may see a branch he wants that is still attached to a tree. Then he flies towards the branch at full speed. He hits it with his feet and grabs it as it cracks and breaks away from the tree.

The male takes each stick he finds to his mate. She is usually the one who builds the nest. She arranges the sticks into a platform that is supported by several tree branches. The platform is normally five feet (1.5 m) across and two feet (.6 m) deep. Then the male gathers sod, weeds, twigs, moss, or corn stalks to give to the female. These things are formed into a soft bed inside the platform. This same technique is also used for less common cliffside nests.

Once the bed has been made, the nest is almost complete. The eagles have one more task left. One of the pair flies off and quickly returns with a sprig of fresh greenery in its beak. It is usually a branch of pine, but any greenery will do. It is then laid inside the nest as if for decoration. Scientists who study eagles do not know why this bit of greenery is always placed in the nest. It is a strange custom among the bald eagles and some other birds of prey. Scientists doubt that it has any practical value to the birds.

15

Repairing the nest

Each spring the eagle couple will return to this same nest. As the nest ages, the floor begins to decay. This calls for constant repairing by the eagles. Each spring new materials are added to the weakened nest floor. One old eagle nest in Florida was measured to be nine and a half feet (2.9 m) wide and twenty feet (6.2 m) deep! Eventually the nests become too heavy for the tree to support. Finally the branches holding it up break, and the nest crashes to the ground. The eagle couple must then build a new one.

From nest to nursery

Once the nest has been completed, it is time to put it to use. Nest building activities of an eagle pair are accompanied by courtship and mating routines.

When the two eagles have mated in their nest, it is only a few days before the first egg is laid. In a few more days one more egg usually will be laid. Occasionally a third egg is laid, but normally the female lays a total of only two eggs. This is the only clutch, or batch, of eggs the female will lay during the year.

The first egg has been laid.

She immediately begins sitting on her eggs to keep them warm. This is called incubation. During incubation the chick inside the egg grows from a tiny speck to an eaglet.

The bald eagle's egg is plain white. It is only slightly bigger than a chicken egg, which seems small for such a large bird. The ends of the egg are bluntly rounded, and the shell is very thick. The two parents take turns sitting on the eggs. While one sits on the eggs, the other will hunt for the pair's daily food. After forty days of incubation, the baby eaglets are ready to hatch.

Breaking through the thick egg shell is hard work for the baby birds. The blind and struggling eaglet chips away at the inside surface of the egg with its egg tooth to free itself. An eaglet's egg tooth is a sharp point on the end of its beak. The baby bird uses this point to gradually chip its way out of the egg. (As, the birds grow up, this egg tooth disappears.) The eaglets hatch from their eggs several days apart from one another, in the order in which they were laid. The parents share the tasks of feeding and caring for the baby chicks.

An eaglet uses the egg tooth at the end of its beak to break out of the egg.

Population Control

Because the female eagle lays her eggs a few days apart, her eaglets hatch a few days apart. Therefore, the young in a nest vary in size. The first hatched eaglet is often quite a bit larger than the one or two eaglets born after it. It always has first choice of the food that its parents bring back to the nest. In a nest of three eaglets, many times the two older baby eagles stay well fed, while the third goes hungry. It is not uncommon for only two eaglets out of three to survive. The third eaglet often starves to death. Occasionally, even in a nest of only two eaglets, the younger will starve.

The parent eagles do not starve these eaglets on purpose. But, the larger eaglets catch most of their attention because of their size. These eaglets are also able to push the weaker one away as they devour most of the food. If the parents bring enough food to the nest, all of the eaglets may survive.

It may seem strange that not all the eaglets are able to survive. However, this is a way in which nature controls the bald eagle population. The bald eagle has no natural enemies. Hawks and tree-climbing snakes would dine on baby eagles if they could, but parent eagles are very protective of their babies. One of them stays with the young at all times. There is little chance of an eaglet falling prey to another animal. It is the fact that small numbers of eagles' offspring survive that keeps the birds from becoming too numerous.

Before people populated the areas in which these birds live, the eagle population remained stable, or constant. However, hunting and the use of insecticides have reduced the natural number of eagles. Now, the fact that only two eaglets per nest usually survive may harm, rather than benefit the eagle.

Growth of the eaglets

When the eaglets hatch, their bodies are covered with thick, soft, smoky-gray down. Their heads are covered with white down. Their eyes are closed, and they are very thin. During this time the eaglets are closely guarded by their parents. They sleep or eat much of the time. The parents tear off tiny bits of food from the prey they bring back to the nest. Then they use their beaks to put the food bits into the baby birds' open mouths.

Three weeks after the eaglets are born their eyes open, and they begin to lose their soft gray down. A darker and thicker down now takes its place. The baby eagles also begin to move about the nest. They brace themselves with their wing tips, for they are not yet able to stand. The eaglets move about with wobbly steps. They begin to peck at the food their parents bring, trying to tear off small pieces to eat. The eaglets are still weak, though, and their parents must still tear the meat for them.

An adult feeds a three-day-old eaglet.

Dark feathers begin replacing the eaglets' down when they are six to seven weeks old. The feathers first appear on their wings and tail. Then they cover their entire bodies. The baby eagles also lose their white head feathers. The new feathers are dark brown, almost black, and it becomes hard to distinguish them as bald eagles.

At this time the eaglets grow very quickly. Their beaks are large and strong. They are now able to tear off pieces of meat for themselves. The young birds quickly grow to full size, and by the time they are nine to ten weeks old, they are as large as their parents. The large nest now becomes quite crowded.

When the eaglets are ten weeks old, they are able to leave the nest. They perch on the edge of the nest and leap several feet into the air. Then they spread their wings and soar for a short time. After practicing several times, they are able to stay in the air for as long as they want. The eaglets hover directly above the nest, though. They are afraid to stray too far.

The mother and father eagles lure their offspring from the nest by placing bits of food at long distances away. The eaglets gradually leave the safety of home and fly toward the pieces of prey. Soon they leave the nest without fear. Then they accompany their parents on hunting flights. They watch as their mother and father dive for fish, ducks and small animals. By the time fall arrives, the young eagles can hunt and kill prey for themselves. They often go

22

A young eagle and one of its parents leave for a hunting trip.

off on hunting flights of their own. The young eagles still sleep in the nest with their parents, but are independent in all other ways.

Time to go south

Then one day the temperatures drop, and ice begins to form on the northern lakes. The bald eagles of the north take to the air for their winter migration.

The path that the eagles fly each fall, as they head

south, may vary. However, hundreds of eagles may follow the same route. This route changes as new food sources become available to the eagles. In recent years an increasing number of eagles have been stopping for food and rest along the Mississippi river. This river runs north and south through the United States from the Great Lakes Region to the Gulf of Mexico. Fish and ducks are more abundant in the river now than they used to be. Eagles have been taking advantage of this new food supply as they migrate to the south.

Parents and eaglets begin the flight together. But, as the family flies south, the young eagles stray farther away from their parents. Eventually they leave their mother and father for good. By the time the parents reach the south and find a place to roost, their offspring have gone off on their own. It will be two or three years before the young eagles look for a mate, and raise their own families.

The journey ends

After a long journey, the migrating eagles finally find an area that is warm enough year-round to have a constant supply of food. Then they stop to spend the winter. The entire southeast corner of the United States is inhabited each year by eagles that have come to spend the winter. The wooded areas along the lower half of the Mississippi river are also favorite winter homes for many eagles. Some of the eagles in these areas are year-round residents. But most are migrants from the North. Some eagles also migrate to the western coast of the United States.

Winter — a time for leisure

Life for the eagle in the winter is less work. There are no young eagles to care for. Despite this, life in the winter is much the same as it is in the summer for the eagles. However, those eagles that have migrated to the South have one thing missing. They have no nests. Since the main purpose of the nest is to be a

In the winter, eagles don't use nests. They roost in tree tops.

place to raise baby eaglets, there is no need for nests in the winter. These homeless birds spend their winter nights sitting, or roosting, in tall tree tops. They sleep throughout the nights, and then, in the early mornings, they fly alone or in pairs to their favorite hunting spots. After a morning of hunting they return to their roosting spots for dinner.

Eagles spend their afternoons relaxing in the trees or flying lazily through the sky. At times eagle mates play games with each other. Several scientists have seen pairs of eagles taking turns at dropping sticks from high in the air. One eagle drops the stick, and its mate flies after it and tries to catch it in the air. The two may continue this game for several minutes.

Time to head home

At last the temperatures begin to rise again as spring approaches. The migrant eagles know it is time to return to the North. Young eagles without mates return to spend their days in much the same way as they did throughout the winter. Eagle pairs return to the nests that they have lived in for many years. Soon they will be busy once again raising the next generation of bald eagles.

A change of color

It will be four or five years before the young eagles look like bald eagles. Each spring eagles molt. This means that their old, worn-out feathers are replaced by new ones. When eagles molt for the first time, their dark brown feathers are replaced by light brown feathers. A few white feathers also emerge in no particular pattern across their bodies. On their fourth or fifth molting, new white feathers cover their entire heads and tails and they have an adult bald eagle's coloration. They keep this color pattern the rest of their lives.

Eagles return to the North before there are leaves on the trees.

CHAPTER THREE:

Fish eagles

Bald eagles rarely prey upon large land animals. In fact, they seldom eat the smaller land animals. Although they do eat an abundance of waterfowl, the main part of their diet consists of fish. Since they eat a lot of fish scientists have nicknamed them "fish eagles."

Seventy to ninety percent of the bald eagle's diet is fish. When fish are not available, eagles eat ducks, turtles, rabbits, squirrels, mice, and other small animals.

The bald eagle goes hunting nearly every day. In the early morning it rises from the nest which it shares with its mate. If there are young ones in the nest, one parent will stay behind to care for the young while the other hunts for food. Young adult eagles which have no mate also hunt alone.

Hunting for fish

When an eagle starts its hunt, it flies to a wooded lake or river. It may fly a dozen miles or so until it

When it is hunting, an eagle perches in a tall tree.

finds a lake where it would like to hunt. Then the eagle perches itself in a tall tree where it can look over the water. It looks with sharp eyes for any dead fish that might be floating in the lake. Eagles can dive into the water and catch live fish, but this is hard work for such a large bird. It is much easier for the eagle to snatch up a dead fish from the top of the water. If the eagle spies such a fish, it immediately swoops down and grabs it with its talons. Then it carries it off to its nest. Eagles always take any prey that they can carry back to their nest.

Food from the osprey

Should the eagle not be able to find any dead fish, it will sit on its perch and watch for an osprey, or other fish-eating birds, to come along.

The eagle waits until an osprey, or another bird, has caught a fish and is flying off with it. Then the bald eagle makes its move. It flies toward the other bird at top speed. It dives down toward the smaller bird, ready to strike with its talons. The eagle screams loudly and repeats its attacks until the bird drops the fish and flies to safety.

Sometimes, instead of attacking the osprey, the eagle may use a different approach. It may swoop beneath the osprey and force the bird to fly higher. Eventually the small bird gets tired of carrying its fish and drops it. Then the eagle dives after the falling fish. It may catch up to the fish and grab onto it in mid air!

Hunting for ducks

On days when the fishing is poor, the eagle might hunt for ducks. It may attack a duck that is on the water, or it may chase one down in the sky. An eagle

An eagle attacks a duck on the water.

that chases a duck through the air usually catches up to it. When it is very close, the eagle will sweep beneath it. Then the eagle will roll over onto its back beneath the duck and thrust its large and powerful talons into the breast of its prey. As soon as the

An eagle has strong talons.

talons touch the duck, a reflex occurs. The talons pull tightly shut in an unbreakable grip. The duck dies instantly, and the eagle rolls back over and flies off to its nest.

Often times a duck is sitting on the water when the eagle first spies it. Then the eagle will fly repeatedly at the duck, forcing it to dive under the water for protection several times. Eventually the duck becomes too tired to dive anymore and the eagle can grab it from the water.

Hunting together

Many times an eagle will hunt with its mate. The two work together with perfect timing. When one of the pair spies a duck on the water, it will swoop at the bird forcing it to dive into the water. Then, just as the duck comes back up, the other eagle swoops at it from the other direction. The duck has no time to catch its breath. By the time the duck surfaces for the second time, the first eagle is ready to strike again. By taking turns, the two eagles force their prey to remain almost constantly under the water. Eventually, the duck has no choice but to emerge from the water long enough to catch its breath. When it does, one of the eagles swoops down and seizes it with its talons. Then the pair of eagles fly back to their nest together and share the meal.

An eagle has a powerful beak.

The two birds may also take turns diving at an osprey that is in flight with a fish. Usually the osprey gives up its fish, and one of the eagles snatches it out of the air and carries it home.

Feeding in winter

Eagles that migrate to the southern United States continue their diet of fish and ducks. Eagles that nest in Alaska and northern Canada spend the winter in southwestern Canada and along the west coast of the United States. Here the coastal waters remain open for some fishing. Eagles in these areas supplement their diet with small land animals as well.

Squirrels, turtles, and rabbits are the most common land prey for the eagles. It catches these animals by swooping down on them from the sky. Since the eagle is not adapted to running on land, it must chase the prey from the air. Eventually the prey becomes tired, and the eagle can grab it with its talons. This is a lot of work for the eagle though. It would much rather hunt for fish or waterfowl, which contain more meat and are easier to catch.

There have been rare cases of larger animals, such as deer and antelope, being eaten by eagles. The eagles kill these animals by piercing them with their large talons. These talons are two to four inches (5-10 cm) long, and are fatal even to a large animal when thrust into its neck or breast. Such attacks by eagles on large animals usually occur during the winter when fishing is poor. Only pairs of eagles kill large animals. A single eagle never attacks such large prey.

CHAPTER FOUR:

The symbol of a nation

On July 4, 1776, the Declaration of Independence was signed by the members of the Continental Congress of the United States. The United States became an independent nation. The members of congress discussed the matter and agreed that a national emblem which showed the strength and independence of the United States should be adopted.

At the end of six years they had come up with nothing. So Congress asked its secretary, Charles Thomson, to come up with a design for the new seal. Thomson worked closely with artist William Barton. The two men created a design of a bald eagle. In one talon the fierce looking eagle carried an olive branch, a symbol of peace. In the other talon the bird held a bundle of arrows, a symbol of strength. Congress quickly adopted the new design as the Great Seal of the United States.

Most of the members of congress were pleased with the new seal. But Benjamin Franklin did not approve of the eagle design. He expressed his dislike of the bald eagle in a letter he wrote to his daughter in 1784: ". . . he is a bird of bad moral character; he does not get his living honestly; you may see him perched on some dead tree, where, too lazy to fish

A drawing of the Great Seal of the United States.

for himself, he watches the labor of the fishing-hawk; when that diligent bird has at length taken a fish, and is bearing it to his nest for the support of his mate and young ones, the bald eagle pursues him and takes it from him." Franklin felt that the wild turkey would have made a much better national seal.

Without trees, there can be no eagles!

An endangered bird

In recent years, people have shown a growing concern over the bald eagle's safety and welfare. However, this has not always been the case.

When the pioneers of America settled this land, they cut down millions of trees. Fields had to be

cleared for crops and lumber was needed to build houses. Little attention was paid to the eagles who lived in the trees. As the number of standing trees decreased across America, so did the number of bald eagles.

In the mid 1900's another factor came into play against the eagles. Humans began using a chemical called DDT (Dichloro-Diphenyl-Trichloroethane). DDT is a powerful insecticide that kills insects. Farmers and government agencies used DDT to control unwanted pests.

After several years of use, DDT began affecting the bald eagle populations of North America. It was carried into streams, rivers, and eventually oceans, by rainwater that ran over the lands where the chemical had been sprayed. Fish that swam in the polluted water breathed the DDT into their bodies through their gills. Soon DDT built up in the fishes' bodies.

Over the years bald eagles ate so many of these fish that DDT began to build up in their bodies, too. The chemical had an unusual effect on the female birds once it was inside them. It made them unable to lay normal eggs. Instead of laying thick, hard shelled eggs, the contaminated females laid eggs with soft, thin shells. The eggs had such soft shells, that when the mother sat on them to incubate them, they broke. During the 1960's and 1970's, many bald eagles were laying these soft-shelled eggs. Some still are today.

Because of DDT, many eagles hatched during the 1960's and 1970's were infertile.

This is not the only effect DDT had on eagles. Some eggs were laid with hard enough shells, but the eaglets that hatched from them were often infertile, and unable to have babies of their own.

During these years, the bald eagle population declined rapidly in North America. The decline was most drastic across the United States, for this was the area where DDT was used the most.

Hope for the eagle

Hope came for the bald eagle in the early 1970's, when the people of the United States began to realize that their national symbol was in trouble. They began making moves to protect the bald eagle from extinction.

An example of people's growing concern occurred in Florida. When highway planners were building Interstate 75 along Florida's west coast, they found that the new road was blocked by a large pine tree. Normally, the tree would have been cut down and the road would have continued straight ahead. But, this pine tree held a giant eagle's nest that was occupied by two eagles. The road builders discussed the problem and decided to build the road around the eagle tree. They gave the interstate a graceful curve and built it three hundred feet away from the nest. This was the first, and perhaps the only time, a road had been built around an eagle nest!

Another example of people's concern for eagles occurred in October of 1971. A gentleman was driving his car along a busy Florida expressway. Suddenly the car in front of him struck a bald eagle. The bird lay stunned in the busy traffic. The man stopped his car and began directing traffic around the injured eagle. Then he picked up the crumpled bird, laid it in his car, and drove to the nearby office of the Audubon Society. The Audubon Society is a group of people who work to protect wild birds in the United States. Doctors were called to the office to care for the eagle, and nine days later the bird had recovered. Newsmen watched with their cameras as the young eagle was set free.

Such incidents of concern for the bald eagle occurred throughout the United States during the 1970's.

Many injured eagles have been healed at special treatment centers.

Even before that time, government agencies worked for the preservation of the bald eagle. In the late 1960's, the bald eagle was placed on the endangered species list by the U.S. Government. This meant that it became illegal to kill the bird. Bird sanctuaries were set up across Florida, so the bald eagle could live at peace in its own natural environment.

Then, in 1972, the use of DDT was banned in the United States.

Making a comeback

Today, there are no large-scale recovery programs for the bald eagle in the United States or Canada. In other words, no special attempts are being made by conservationists to greatly increase the number of eagles. It seems that such programs are not needed. Recent counts of bald eagles across North America show that the birds are definitely making a comeback.

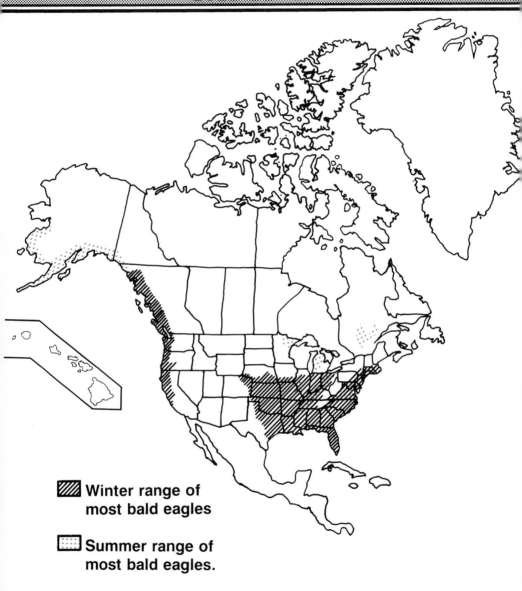

Winter range of
most bald eagles

Summer range of
most bald eagles.

INDEX/GLOSSARY:

READ AND ENJOY THE SERIES:

THE
WHITETAIL • THE **PHEASANT**

THE
BALD EAGLE • THE **WOLVES**

THE
SQUIRRELS • THE **BEAVER**

THE
GRIZZLY • THE **MALLARD**

THE
RACCOON • THE **WILD CATS**

THE
RATTLESNAKE • THE **SHEEP**

THE
ALLIGATOR • THE **CARIBOU**

THE
CANADA GOOSE • THE **FOXES**